Kingdom Kids Learn To Write!

Alphabet Edition

For Parents

By the age of 4, most children have gained enough motor control to clench a crayon or pencil and draw wavy lines. At this age they are attempting to write letters, especially the ones in their name. This book will help your child develop their writing skills while also exposing them to the full alphabet and The Bible!

Exposing your child to scripture is important even at this age. Incorporating memory verses as they learn how to write their alphabets is a fun way to introduce and create a desire for God's word! Train up a child in the way they should go and they will not depart from it (Prov 22:6).

Remember that repetition is key! Whether you are going through the memory verse or having your Kingdom Kid practice their writing, do it over and over!

Name:

Above all else guard your
heart for it is a wellspring
of life
- Proverbs 4:23

Aa Aa Aa Aa Aa

Aa Aa Aa Aa Aa

Aa Aa Aa Aa Aa

Name:

Believe in the Lord Jesus
Christ and you will be
saved
- Acts 16:31

Bb Bb Bb Bb Bb

Bb Bb Bb Bb Bb

Bb Bb Bb Bb Bb

Name:

Children obey your parents
in the Lord, for this is right
- Ephesians 6:1

Cc   Cc   Cc   Cc   Cc

Cc   Cc   Cc   Cc   Cc

Cc   Cc   Cc   Cc   Cc

Do everything without
complaining or arguing
- Philippians 2:14

Dd Dd Dd Dd Dd

Dd Dd Dd Dd Dd

Dd Dd Dd Dd Dd

Name:

Encourage one another
and build each other up
- 1 Thessalonians 5:11

Name:

Fear not for I am with you
- Isaiah 43:5

Name:

God is Love
- 1 John 4:8

Gg Gg Gg Gg Gg

Gg Gg Gg Gg Gg

Gg Gg Gg Gg Gg

Name:

Honor thy Father and thy Mother
- Exodus 20:12

Hh   Hh   Hh   Hh   Hh

Hh   Hh   Hh   Hh   Hh

Hh   Hh   Hh   Hh   Hh

Name:

If God is for us, who can be against us
- Romans 8:31

Jesus answered, "I am the
way and the truth and the
life. No one comes to the
Father except through me.
- John 14:6

Name:

Keep your tongue from evil
and your lips from telling
lies
- Psalms 34:13

Kk Kk Kk Kk Kk

Kk Kk Kk Kk Kk

Kk Kk Kk Kk Kk

Love the Lord your God
with all your heart and
with all your soul and with
all your strength
- Deuteronomy 6:5

Name:

Make a joyful noise unto the
Lord
- Psalms 98:4

Mm   Mm   Mm   Mm   Mm

Mm   Mm   Mm   Mm   Mm

Mm   Mm   Mm   Mm   Mm

Name:

Nothing is impossible with
God
- Luke 1:37

Name:

Oh, give thanks to the Lord,
for He is good!
For His mercy endures
forever.
- Psalm 136:1

Name:

Peace I leave with you, my
peace I give to you
- John 14:27

Pp Pp Pp Pp Pp

Pp Pp Pp Pp Pp

Pp Pp Pp Pp Pp

Name:

Quick to listen, slow to
speak, and slow to
become angry.
- James 1:19

Qq   Qq   Qq   Qq   Qq

Qq   Qq   Qq   Qq   Qq

Qq   Qq   Qq   Qq   Qq

Rejoice in the Lord always;
again I will say, rejoice!
- Philippians 4:4

Seek first His kingdom and
His righteousness, and all
these things will be added
to you.
-Matthew 6:33

Ss Ss Ss Ss Ss

Ss Ss Ss Ss Ss

Ss Ss Ss Ss Ss

Name:

Trust in the Lord with all
your heart and lean not
on your own
understanding
- Proverbs 3:5

Understanding is a fountain
of life to one who has it.
- Proverbs 16:22

Name:

Very early in the morning, while it
was still dark, Jesus got up, left the
house and went off to a solitary
place,
where he prayed.
- Mark 1:35

Name:

When I am afraid I will trust
in you
- Psalms 56:3

Name:

eXalt thyself O God
above the heavens
- Psalms 108:5

Name:

You are the light of the
world
- Matthew 5:14

Y y   Y y   Y y   Y y   Y y

Y y   Y y   Y y   Y y   Y y

Y y   Y y   Y y   Y y   Y y

Name:

Zacchaeus, come down
immediately. I must stay
at your house today.
- Luke 19:5